Drizzle On The Way

Anusha Kostka

BookLeaf Publishing

India | USA | UK

Presentation by *BookLeaf Publishing*

Web: www.bookleafpub.com

E-mail: info@bookleafpub.com

ISBN: 9789363311787

First edition 2024

ACKNOWLEDGEMENT

"To all who inspire my dreams and keep my heart warm amidst life's gentle drizzle of pages turned, this poem is lovingly dedicated."

As I embark on this journey of words and thoughts, I find myself compelled to express my deepest gratitude to those who have been the pillars of my life—the guiding lights that have illuminated my path and the gentle rain that has nourished my soul.

First and foremost, I owe an immense debt of gratitude to my parents. Their unwavering love, boundless support, and invaluable wisdom have shaped me into the person I am today. Their encouragement to explore the realms of imagination and knowledge has been a constant source of inspiration.

I also extend my heartfelt thanks to my husband, whose unwavering belief in my abilities has been a source of strength. His encouragement and understanding have been the cornerstone of my creative endeavors.

To all my family members at home, whose presence brings joy and warmth to my days, I am grateful beyond words. Your love and encouragement have been a source of motivation and comfort throughout this journey.

Last but not least, I express my gratitude to you, dear reader, for embarking on this literary voyage with me. It is my sincere hope that the words within these pages resonate with you and bring a spark of joy, reflection, or inspiration to your life.

PREFACE

Dear Reader,

Welcome to "Drizzle on the Way," a collection of poetry that seeks to capture the essence of life's myriad emotions and experiences. As you delve into these verses, you'll find a journey through moments of joy, sorrow, love, and longing, each woven into the fabric of human existence.

This book is a reflection of my own journey, where words became my companions through the highs and lows of life. It is an exploration of the beauty found in simplicity, the resilience of the human spirit, and the power of hope that guides us through difficult times.

I hope these poems resonate with you, offering comfort, inspiration, and perhaps a mirror to your own experiences. May they remind you that amidst life's storms and drizzles, there is always beauty to be found and moments of grace that light our way.

Thank you for joining me on this poetic voyage. May the pages of "Drizzle on the Way" bring you moments of reflection, connection, and discovery.

With gratitude and warm regards,

Anusha Kostka

Awakening of the Dawn

As the sun rises, I take a stroll,
Among the mulberries, my heart's console.
The air is crisp, the world is calm,
Birds chirp softly, singing a psalm.

Dewdrops glisten on the green,
Flowers bloom, a sight serene.
Mulberries hang, ripe and sweet,
I pluck a few, a morning treat.

Sunbeams filter through the trees,
Warming me with a gentle breeze.
Nature's embrace, so pure and true,
Morning walks, a joy I pursue.

A Sip of Morning's Brew

In the hush of morning's light,
A sip of brew, a pure delight.
Steam rises gently, a comforting sight,
In this moment, everything feels just right.

The aroma swirls, inviting and warm,
A gentle reminder of a new day's form.
Each sip carries flavors, a subtle treat,
Awakening senses, a feeling so sweet.

Coffee or tea, the choice is clear,
Both bring joy, banishing any fear.
With each sip I take, calmness flows,
Embracing the morning as it slowly grows.

So here's to mornings, simple and pure,
And the magic in each cup's allure.
In these quiet sips, I find my way,
Ready to seize the day, come what may.

Secret of the Sky

Beneath a canvas vast and blue,
Where dreams and whispers softly grew,
I find my gaze drawn far and high,
To where the heavens paint their sigh.

In twilight's calm or morning's gleam,
The sky unfolds its timeless dream.
With hues that dance in gentle play,
It steals my breath and holds dismay.

The sun, a golden, blazing fire,
Ignites the day, a grand empire.
Clouds, like ships in silent flight,
Drift across the canvas bright.

At night, the stars, a twinkling choir,
Sing secrets in celestial attire.
Moonbeams weave a silver thread,
Through the dark, where dreams are led.

I stand below, in humble awe,
As sky and earth share whispered law.
For in its vast and endless span,
I see the dreams of mortal man.

So, here I stand, with head held high,
In reverence to the boundless sky.
For in its depths, I find my muse,
And in its beauty, never lose.

Blossom's

Blossoms bloom in soft delight,
Painting spring with colors bright.
Petals whisper in the breeze,
Secrets carried through the trees.

Cherry blossoms, pink and fair,
Scatter beauty everywhere.
Apple blossoms, white as snow,
In orchards where sweet fruits grow.

Lavender blooms with calming scent,
In the gardens, a tranquil event.
Roses blush in shades so deep,
Love's own language, hearts they keep.

Sunflowers rise with faces bold,
Chasing sunlight, never old.
Jasmine's fragrance fills the air,
A melody beyond to compare.

Blossoms sing of life's gentle grace,
In their bloom, a warm embrace.
Nature's art, pure and free,
In blossoms, beauty will always be.

Snow White's Castle

In a land of stories, there's a castle bright,
Where Snow White lived, full of light.

It had tall towers touching the sky,
With windows sparkling, catching the eye.

Inside, a tale of love and joy,
With Snow White, a princess, not a toy.

Her friends were seven dwarves, full of cheer,
They worked together, year after year.

The castle had a magic mirror, it's true,
Speaking truths, helping Snow White through.

But a wicked queen, full of envy and spite,
Tried to harm Snow White with all her might.

Yet love and kindness won in the end,
In Snow White's castle, they'll forever defend.

So remember this tale of love so true,
In a castle bright, skies always blue.

With Tulip's in My Mind…

In gardens bright, tulips grow,
With colors bold in a vibrant show.
They're like soft petals, smooth and fine,
Swinging in the breeze, oh, so divine!

Some are red like fire, burning bright,
Others are pink, a soft delight.
Yellow tulips are happy and cheery,
Their sunny faces never weary.

White tulips are pure, like fresh snow,
Their beauty shines a lovely glow.
Purple ones, like kings, stand tall,
Tulips are loved by one and all.

Their stems are strong, reaching high,
Drinking water as clouds pass by.
In spring, they bloom, a joyful sight,
Tulips bring colors, pure and right.

So, in gardens or by your door,
Tulips bring happiness, that's for sure.
With every petal, a story's spun,
Of love, of life, under the sun.

River's Joy

The river wakes up early, quiet and calm,
It whispers secrets, like a soothing psalm.
In the morning light, it shines so bright,
Reflecting the sun's warmth, a pure delight.

The river tells stories, old and wise,
Of long journeys under open skies.
Through valleys and mountains, it gracefully
flows,
Singing a song that the whole world knows.

In its gentle embrace, troubles disappear,
Leaving behind a sense of cheer.
Birds sing along, trees sway in glee,
As the river dances, wild and free.

The river brings joy, a comforting friend,
Guiding us through until the very end.
Its soft murmur soothes, like a healing balm,
Bringing us peace, bringing us calm.

Through all seasons, the river stays true,
A constant presence, always anew.
Let's treasure its joy, simple and pure,
For the river's beauty will endure.

Wonder's of Nature

Nature's wonders are both big and small,
From towering mountains to creatures so spry.
In lush forests and oceans wide,
Where beauty and magic coincide.

Mountains high with peaks of snow,
Whispering winds share tales we know.
Through valleys deep, rivers flow,
Life awakens in nature's show.

The ocean vast, a world unseen,
With creatures unique, a vibrant scene.
Whales sing songs, dolphins play,
In waves that dance throughout the day.

Fields of flowers in colors bright,
Bees buzz happily, a joyful sight.
Butterflies flutter, delicate and free,
Adding grace to the world we see.

The sun's warm rays, a golden gleam,
Stars twinkle softly, a cosmic dream.
Nature's wonders, a timeless treasure,
Reminding us of life's boundless measure.

Let's cherish nature, protect its grace,
For its wonders bring joy to every place.
In every breeze, in every tree,
We find a world that's wild and free.

Merry Go Round

In the park, as the sun starts to set,
Children gather, filled with joy and zest.
A spinning merry-go-round, with horses so
grand,
They jump on eagerly, hand in hand.

Round and round, the merry-go-round turns,
Their giggles and laughter, the music that
churns.
On painted horses, they ride so free,
Imagining adventures, wild as can be.

With each spin, dreams take flight,
In their eyes, the world shines bright.
They reach for the sky, full of glee,
A whirl of childhood's pure ecstasy.

Oh, the merry-go-round of childhood's fun,
Underneath the golden sun,
Kids play and laugh, their hearts unfurled,
On this spinning, magical world.

The Gentle Breeze

The gentle breeze, it softly blows,
Through trees and fields, it calmly flows.
Like a whisper, light and kind,
It brings us peace, a gentle find.

It dances with the leaves and flowers,
Bringing scents from nature's bowers.
It talks to trees; they sway and sing,
A quiet tune that joy can bring.

In summer's heat or winter's cold,
It tells stories, new and old.
It cools our cheeks with a gentle touch,
A moment of calm, it gives so much.

Oh, breeze so gentle, we're glad you're here,
Your quiet presence, so calm and clear.
You soothe our hearts, you ease our day,
In your embrace, we find our way.

The Windmill In My Town

In the heart of our quaint town, a windmill
stands tall,
Its sails spin gracefully, a rhythmic dance for all.
A symbol of our history, a guardian of the past,
Whispering tales of old memories that forever
last.

With each gentle breeze, it comes alive,
A majestic spectacle that makes us thrive.
Its wooden arms reach for the endless sky,
A timeless beauty that never says goodbye.

In the morning light, it's a sight to behold,
A beacon of hope, a story untold.
As the sun sets, casting shadows long,
The windmill sings its tranquil song.

Through seasons of change, it stands the test,
A steadfast sentinel, never at rest.
In summer's warmth or winter's chill,
The windmill stands proud, serene, and still.

Oh, the windmill of our town, we cherish thee,
A symbol of strength, a sight to see.
Forever in our hearts, your spirit reigns,
A timeless symbol of our rustic plains.

Seashell's

In the sands of time, where whispers dwell,
Lies treasures of the ocean's spell.
Seashells, delicate and fair,
Stories in each curve they bear.

Upon the shore, they lay in peace,
Gifts from waves that never cease.
Pearlescent wonders, nature's art,
Capturing dreams, a world apart.

Listen closely, hear the sea's song,
In every shell, where echoes belong.
Tales of journeys, far and wide,
In colors, patterns, they confide.

From spiral dances to conchs so grand,
Infinite beauty, grains of sand.
Whispers of tides, secrets untold,
In these shells, mysteries unfold.

Carved by time, with love and grace,
Mirrors of the ocean's embrace.
Seashells, oh how they inspire,
A symphony of nature's choir.

Hold them close, hear their story,
A tribute to the sea's vast glory.
In every shell, a journey begins,
A testament to where the ocean wins.

Rhythm

Rhythm is like a hidden drum,
Beating with life, never feeling glum.
In every sound, it plays its part,
Guiding us along, from the very start.

It flows like a river, steady and true,
In everything we do, it shines through.
From a strong heartbeat to a bird's song,
Rhythm keeps us moving all day long.

Tap your feet, feel the beat,
Rhythm's magic, oh so sweet.
It colors our days with joyful tunes,
A dance of life under the sun or moon.

In quiet moments or busy days,
Rhythm guides us in so many ways.
It brings us together in a cheerful rhyme,
A dance of life, a timeless chime.

The Lighthouse

On the rocky shore, a tower stands tall,
It's called a lighthouse, watching over all.
In the dark of night, its light shines bright,
Guiding sailors home, a comforting sight.

With winds that roar and waves that crash,
The lighthouse stays strong; it never lacks.
It's like a friend to ships at sea,
Showing them the way, where they should be.

In the sky, its light dances around,
A signal of safety, a reassuring sound.
Through storms and calm, it never rests,
A protector of sailors, doing its best.

So next time you see a lighthouse's glow,
Remember its purpose, and let it show,
That in life's storms, there's always a guide,
A beacon of hope, with arms open wide.

The Ocean

The ocean near my home,
Where waves gently foam,
A place of peace and play,
Where I love to stay.

The water's deep blue,
With seagulls' cries so true,
They dance in the sky,
As the sun sets by.

Sand under my feet,
Where seashells we meet,
Stories they whisper,
Of the sea's grand picture.

Breezes salty and light,
Bring memories bright,
Of childhood days free,
By the endless sea.

The ocean, a friend so dear,
With secrets to share, never fear,
Its soothing rhythm, a calming song,
In its embrace, I belong.

The Aroma

Before rain begins to fall from above,
The air carries a scent that I dearly love.
Nature softly whispers its secrets near,
Of rain that brings life, so crystal clear.

The breeze brings scents that gently play,
Before rain showers come our way.
Clouds gather, painting the sky so wide,
Ready to quench the earth's thirst with pride.

Every raindrop moves with its own grace,
Bringing life to plants in a gentle embrace.
Leaves shimmer with a hopeful gleam,
Knowing rainwater is like a dream.

The air smells fresh, with rain on its way,
Nature's perfume in the air does sway.
Let's savor this moment, calm and serene,
Before rain turns the earth into a lush green.

The Cloud's Sway Along

In the sky so big and blue,
Clouds float like fluffy white glue,
They gather near the shining sun,
In the morning, the day's just begun.

The sun paints them with golden light,
Making the sky so pure and bright,
Clouds change shapes and start to play,
In the sun's colors, they sway.

They move and shift in the air,
A beautiful sight beyond compare,
The sun's rays make them shine,
In the sky, a show divine.

Watching this movement, it's clear to see,
How beautiful nature can be,
In every sky, big or small,
Beauty's there if we just recall.

Everyone Know's

The sky, deep and wide, hints at a tale,
Whispers secrets as clouds gather, set to unveil.
A silent crowd gathers, the air heavy,
Earth's thirst awaiting the downpour, ready.

The scent of rain hangs, sweet and near,
Leaves rustle, nature's chorus, crystal clear.
Birds chirp their final melodies,
Nature's orchestra before the storm's mysteries.

The world pauses, sensing the change,
Awaiting the blessing, the cleansing rain.
The breeze whispers softly, a tender touch,
Nature's embrace, a prelude, a calm clutch.

Thunder rumbles, a distant drumroll,
The rain's arrival, nature's grand patrol.
In every heart, the anticipation reigns,
As everyone knows, it's about to rain.

A symphony of droplets, a rhythmic way,
Blessing the earth in nature's array.
So everyone knows, without refrain,
That it's about to rain again.

The First Droplet

When the sky gets dark and gray,
And clouds gather quietly in their way,
Nature gets calm, like in a dream,
Getting ready for rain's soft stream.

Birds find trees to hide and rest,
Their chirping quiets, a peaceful nest,
Leaves rustle, a soft whisper in the air,
As raindrops start to gather everywhere.

The air feels heavy, with rain about to fall,
The earth waits eagerly, answering nature's call,
Flowers bend, waiting for the drops to land,
As rain brings life to the earth, so grand.

The first drop falls, a happy sound indeed,
Nature sings, with every drop it needs,
Rivers flow, happy to embrace the rain,
As it nourishes the earth, again and again.

Drizzle

Clouds gather in the sky so high,
A drizzle's whisper, a gentle sigh.
The air feels cool, the breeze does play,
Raindrop's coming, not far away.

Leaves shimmer, wet and bright,
Birds rest, taking a quiet flight.
The world waits, feeling calm and still,
For the rain's touch, a peaceful thrill.

The ground smiles, getting a drink,
As raindrop's fall, a soft link.
Nature's rhythm, in this sweet sound,
A drizzle's arrival, so profound.

Let's enjoy this moment, simple and dear,
The rain's soft touch, drawing near.
In its gentle song, we find a way,
To rest and relax, in the drizzle's sway.

A Window's Tale

Amidst the whispers of the rain's soft patter,
I sit by the window, a silent spectator.
The world outside, veiled in a gentle haze,
As the drizzle weaves its tranquil maze.

Each droplet, a dancer in nature's ballet,
Gracefully pirouetting in its own way.
The scent of wet earth fills the air,
A melody of raindrops, beyond compare.

I watch as nature paints a masterpiece,
With hues of gray and whispers of peace.
The world slows down in the drizzle's embrace,
A moment of serenity, a tranquil space.

The trees sway gently, their leaves adorned,
With glistening jewels, the rain has adorned.
A symphony of tranquility, a sight so divine,
As I watch the drizzle outside, my heart aligns.

In this quiet moment, where time stands still,
I find solace in the rain's gentle thrill.
The world outside may rush and strive,
But here by my window, I feel alive.